# The power of thinking less and doing more

## The art of  Making a move, Executing, and Self-control

# JOHN GREGORY

# TABLE OF CONTENTS

# Chapter 1

**THE ACT OF WORRYING**

Stresses, questions, and nerves are an ordinary piece of life. It's normal to stress over a neglected bill, an impending prospective employee meeting, or a first date. Be that as it may, "ordinary" stress becomes over the top when it's tenacious and wild. You stress consistently over "what uncertainties" and most pessimistic scenario situations, you can't get genuine fears somewhere far away from me, and it obstructs your day-to-day existence.

Steady stressing, pessimistic reasoning, and continuously expecting the most horrendously terrible can negatively affect your profound and actual well-being. It can drain your close-to-home strength, leave you feeling fretful and unsteady, cause a sleeping disorder, cerebral pains, stomach issues, and muscle strain, and make it challenging to gather at work or school.

You might take your gloomy sentiments out on individuals nearest to you, self-sedate with liquor or medications, or attempt to divert yourself by daydreaming before screens. Persistent stressing can likewise be a significant side effect of Summed Uneasiness Problem (Stray), a typical tension issue that includes pressure, apprehension, and a general sensation of disquiet that colors for what seems like forever.

If you're tormented by misrepresented stress and strain, there are steps you can take to switch off fears. Constant stressing is a psychological propensity that can be broken. You can prepare your cerebrum to keep even-tempered and check out at life from a more adjusted, less unfortunate viewpoint.

Address an Authorized Specialist

Steady stress can cause significant damage. It can keep you up around evening time and make you tense and restless during the day. What's more, even though you disdain feeling like a worry wort, it can in any case be so challenging to stop. For most constant worriers, the apprehensions are energized by the convictions — both negative and positive — that you hold about stressing:

Negative convictions about stress. You might accept that your consistent stressing is unsafe, that making you insane or influencing your actual health is going. Or on the other hand, you might stress that you will lose all command over your stressing — that it won't dominate and ever stop. While negative convictions, or agonizing over stressing, add to your nervousness and makes a big difference in stress, positive convictions about stressing can similarly as harmful.

Positive convictions about stress. You might accept that your stressing assists you with keeping away from terrible things, forestalls issues, sets you up for the most terrible, or prompts arrangements. Perhaps you let yourself that know if you continue to stress over an issue sufficiently long, you'll ultimately have the option to sort it out. Or on the other hand, maybe you're persuaded that stressing is something mindful to do or the best way to guarantee you don't disregard something. It's difficult to get out from under the concern propensity if you trust that your stress fills a positive need. When you understand that stressing is the issue, not the arrangement, you can recover control of your stressed brain.

The most effective method to quit stressing tip 1: Make a day-to-day "stress" period
It's hard to be useful in your day-to-day exercises when uneasiness and stress are ruling your contemplations and diverting you from work, school, or your home life. This is where the methodology of deferring stressing can help. Instead of attempting to stop or dispose of fear, allow yourself to have it, yet put off harping on it until some other time.

Make a "stress period." Pick a set setting for stressing. It ought to be similar consistently (for example in the lounge from 5:00 to 5:20 p.m.) and early enough that it won't make you restless just before sleep time. During your concern period, you're permitted to stress over anything that's at the forefront of your thoughts. The remainder of the day, be that as it may, is an effortless zone.

Record your concerns. On the off chance that fear or stress comes into your head during the day, make a concise note of it and afterward go on about your day. Advise yourself that have the opportunity and energy to consider it later, so there's a compelling reason need to stress over it at present. Likewise, recording your contemplations — on a cushion or your telephone or PC — is a lot harder work than basically suspecting them, so your concerns are bound to lose their power.

Go over your "stress list" during the concern time frame. Assuming the considerations you recorded are as yet annoying you, permit yourself to stress over them, however just for how much time you've determined for your concern period. As you look at your concerns along these lines, you'll frequently find it simpler to foster a more adjusted viewpoint. Furthermore, on the off chance that your concerns don't appear to be signing anymore, just cut your concern period off and partake in the remainder of your day.

Tip 2: Challenge feelings of apprehension

Assuming you experience the ill effects of ongoing nervousness and stress, odds are you take a gander at the world in manners that cause it to appear to be more compromising than it truly is. For instance, you might misjudge the likelihood that things will turn out seriously, bounce quickly to most pessimistic scenario situations, or treat each apprehension as though it were reality. You may likewise dishonor your capacity to deal with life's concerns, accepting you'll self-destruct at the earliest difficult situation.

These kinds of considerations, known as mental bends, include:

Win big or bust thinking, seeing things in dark or-white classes, with no center ground. "On the off chance that everything is flawed, I'm an all-out disappointment."

Overgeneralization from a solitary negative encounter, anticipating that it should turn out as expected until the end of time. "I didn't land recruited for the position. I won't ever land any position."

Zeroing in on the negatives while sifting through the upsides. Seeing the one thing that turned out badly, instead of the multitude of things that went right. "I triumphed ultimately the keep going inquiry on the test wrong. I'm an imbecile."

Concocting justifications for why positive occasions don't count. "I excelled on the show, however, that was simply blind chance."

Making negative understandings without real proof. You carry on like telepathic: "I can perceive she covertly despises me." Or a psychic: "I simply know something horrible will occur."

Anticipating that the worst situation imaginable should occur. "The pilot expressed we're in for some choppiness. The plane will crash!"

Accepting that how you feel reflects reality. "I feel like such a blockhead. Everybody should be giggling at me."

Holding yourself to a severe rundown of what you ought to and shouldn't do and thumping yourself on the off chance that you disrupt any of the norms. "I ought to never have had a go at beginning a discussion with her. I'm such a blockhead."

Naming yourself in light of errors and seeing deficiencies. "I'm a disappointment; I'm exhausting; I should be separated from everyone else."

Taking care of things that are beyond your reach.
"It's my issue my child got in a mishap. I ought
to have cautioned him to drive cautiously in the
downpour."

The most effective method to challenge these
contemplations
During your concern period, challenge your
negative considerations by asking yourself:

The fact that the idea is valid makes what the
proof? That it's false?
Is there a more sure, reasonable perspective on
circumstance?
What's the likelihood that what I'm frightened of
will occur? Assuming the likelihood is low, what
are a few additional reasonable results?
Is the idea accommodating? How might
stressing over it assist me and how will it hurt
me?
What might I share with this companion stress?
Tip 3: Recognize resolvable and unsolvable
concerns

Research shows that while you're stressing, you briefly feel less restless. Running over the issue in your mind occupies you from your feelings and causes you to feel like you're getting something achieved. However, stressing and critical thinking are two altogether different things.

Critical thinking includes assessing what is happening, concocting substantial strides for managing it, and afterward setting the strategy in motion. Stressing, then again, seldom prompts arrangements. Regardless of how long you spend harping on most pessimistic scenario situations, you're not any more ready to manage them would it be advisable for them if they occur?

Is your concern reasonable?
Useful, reasonable concerns are those you can make a move on immediately. For instance, if you're stressed over your bills, you could call your leasers to see about adaptable installment choices. Inefficient, unsolvable concerns are those for which there is no related activity.

"Consider the possibility that I get a disease sometime in the not-so-distant future?" or "Imagine a scenario in which my child gets into a mishap."

On the off chance that the concern is resolvable, begin conceptualizing. Create a rundown of the multitude of potential arrangements you can imagine. Make an effort not to get too hung up on tracking down the ideal arrangement. Center around the things you can change, as opposed to the conditions or real factors unchangeable as far as you might be concerned. After you've assessed your choices, arrange the activity. When you have an arrangement and begin taking care of the issue, you'll feel significantly less restless.

If the concern isn't resolvable, acknowledge the vulnerability. If you're a constant worrier, by far most of your fears presumably fall in this camp. Stressing is much of the time a way we attempt to foresee what's to come in store-a method for forestalling disagreeable shocks and controlling the result. The issue is, it doesn't work. Contemplating everything that could turn out badly doesn't make life any more unsurprising. Zeroing in on most pessimistic scenario situations will just hold you back from partaking in the beneficial things you have in the present. To quit stressing, tackle your requirement for assurance and quick responses.

Do you will more often than not anticipate terrible things will happen because they are questionable? What is the probability they will? Given the probability is extremely low, is it conceivable to live with the little opportunity that something negative might occur?
Ask your loved ones how they adapt to vulnerability in unambiguous circumstances. Might you at some point do likewise?
Tune into your feelings. Stressing over vulnerability is many times a method for staying away from horrendous feelings. Yet, by tuning into your feelings you can begin to acknowledge your sentiments, even those that are awkward or don't appear to be legit.

Tip 4: Interfere with the concerned cycle
Assuming you stress unnecessarily, it can seem
like negative considerations are going through
your mind on unending rehash. You might feel
like you're spiraling wild, going off the deep
end, or going to wear out unde

# Chapter 2

**HOW TO STEP UP AND FOCUS**

We've all been there: sitting in your work area with a pressing cutoff time and a meandering brain. Despite your earnest attempts, things are not advancing. You want to zero in on the undertaking before you. You're roused to make it happen. In any case, you can't focus.

In this computerized world, we are quickly drawn off track. Data is all over the place and we want to manage expanding and different types of data. It delays our time and our consideration.

The powerlessness to focus on the job needing to be done is one of the diseases within recent memory - everybody needs to know how to concentrate better, and how to think. However, the advantages of further developing fixation and center make it an issue worth tending to.

What is the focus?

In Resolution and Self-control, Remez Sasson composed that fixation is the capacity to guide one's consideration following one's will. Fixation implies control of consideration. It is the capacity to zero in the psyche on one subject, article, or thought, and simultaneously prohibit from the brain every other irrelevant idea, thought, sentiment, and sensation.

That last part is the interesting part for a large portion of us. To focus is to reject, or not focus on, every other inconsequential idea, thought, feeling, or sensation. To not focus on the numbers, blares, and different markers we have another message, another update, a new "like," another devotee!

Our everyday schedule is overwhelmed by exchanging all through our cell phones and PC. We get a steady deluge of messages from WhatsApp, email, Wire, and about six other applications that are some way or another basic to our work. We continually look for data to assist with tackling our day-to-day issues or finishing our work.

Successive interruptions influence efficiency. It takes more time to complete a responsibility. We don't tune in also. We don't appreciate things also, whether with our accomplices or with partners, and end up in misconception, confusion, and struggle. It influences memory. We fail to remember things or can't remember data immediately which influences our own life and expert picture.

Factors influencing fixation
Every so often it seems like our focus is enduring an onslaught from all sides. Fixation is impacted by both inside and outer or natural variables. If you have any desire to figure out how to further develop concentration and memory, it assists with grasping what's disrupting everything now.

Interruption. We are barraged by a consistent progression of data, whether new or old, during the method involved with following through with something. Analysts possess observed that our brainpower is so prepared for this interruption that simply seeing our cell phone impedes our capacity to think. We continually survey whether the data is helpful, adequate, or insignificant. The sheer amount coming in jumbles our evaluation of whether we need more data to simply decide.

Deficient rest. Researchers have found that the absence of rest can prompt lower readiness, more slow perspectives, and decreased focus. You will have more trouble concentrating and may end up being befuddled. Therefore, your capacity to perform errands, particularly connecting with thinking or rationale can be truly impacted. Constantly unfortunate rest further influences your focus and memory. Dr. Allison T. Siebern from the Stanford College Rest Medication Center notes that on the off chance that you can't focus on what is within reach, coming to either your short-or long haul memory is far-fetched.

Inadequate active work. Have you at any point seen how incredible activity leaves you feeling more loose and vivacious over the day? At the point when you don't do actual work, your muscles can become tense. You might feel snugness in your neck, shoulder, and chest and such relentless, low-level distress can influence your fixation.

Dietary patterns. What we eat adds to how we feel, including our smartness and lucidity, for the day. If we don't fuel our minds with the appropriate supplements, we begin to encounter side effects like cognitive decline, exhaustion, and absence of focus. Low-fat eating regimens can demolish the center because the cerebrum needs specific fundamental unsaturated fats. Other prohibitive eating regimens may adversely influence fixation by not giving the supplements the cerebrum needs or by making appetite, desires, or sensations of unwellness in the body that are themselves diverting.

Climate. Contingent to what you are doing, the climate can influence your concentration. A commotion level that is too clear is an issue,

however many individuals likewise experience issues concentrating when it is excessively calm. It isn't simply the general clamor level yet the kind of clamor that is important: the high-energy, mysterious murmur of a café could bring center while the heard discussion of two collaborators crashes it. A main tune rapidly makes them chime in, joyfully diverted, while less particular instrumentals could keep you sensitive to the errand. Lighting that is too splendid or too faint can influence your vision. A room that is too hot or too cold makes distress.
These components can influence your fixation. Joyfully, they are additionally all addressable.

Conditions connected with focus
On the off chance that you often can't concentrate on your considerations and are encountering progressing fixation challenges, it might show a mental, clinical, mental, way of life or ecological reason. Contingent upon the reason, you might need to briefly acknowledge that your focus is low and gain proficiency with a couple of stunts to diminish the effect or

acknowledge the plunges. If you want assistance with fixation and think your troubles go past the rundown above, talk with an expert.

Conceivable more extensive circumstances include:

Mental. Your fixation might diminish assuming you find yourself failing to remember things without any problem. Your memory here and their bombs you, you lose articles, and experience issues recalling things that happened a brief time frame prior. Another way your focus might be intellectually debilitated is assuming you observe that your brain is overactive continually thinking about different things because of worries or significant occasions. At the point when considerations and issues barge into you, requesting consideration, it forestalls powerful focus.

Mental. At the point when you are discouraged and feeling down, it is challenging to center. Essentially, when you are recuperating from the departure of a friend or family member during mourning or are encountering tension, you might experience issues zeroing in on a solitary errand.

Clinical. Ailments like diabetes, hormonal uneven characters, and low red platelet count can influence our fixation. Some drug likewise makes you sleepy or dim and seriously impede fixation.

Climate. Unfortunate working circumstances, shared spaces, and extreme or negative work elements may likewise add to an absence of focus. At the point when we are encountering burnout or stress from work or individual life, we will find it challenging to think because of close-to-home fatigue. Essentially, the climate can make inconvenience our body with impacts that we're mindful of (heat, light, commotion) and others that don't completely enlist (strain, cynicism, checking).

Way of life. Exhaustion, yearning, and parchedness can wreck focus. Ways of life that include too many missed dinners, rich food varieties, or unnecessary liquor utilization can provoke our memory and capacity to think and concentrate.

15 Methods for working on your focus

Presently you know why you want assistance with fixation. What can assist you with centering better? There's nobody reply for how to further develop concentration, yet the accompanying tips can help.

Dispense with interruptions. How improve on the off chance that we are constantly assaulted with data? Make training to impede time in your timetable to do a particular errand or action. During this time, demand that you be let be or go to where others are probably not going to upset you: a library, a café, a confidential room.

Close virtual entertainment and other applications, quiet warnings, and keep your telephone stowed away from sight in a sack or rucksack. As depicted in HBR, analysts observed that mental limit was altogether better when the telephone was hidden, not simply switched off. Maintain Your essential center is to finish what you want to do. Stopping both inward and outside aggravations can assist you with concentrating.

Diminish performing multiple tasks. Endeavoring to play out numerous exercises simultaneously causes us to feel useful. It's likewise a recipe for a lower center, unfortunate focus, and lower efficiency. What's more, lower efficiency can prompt burnout. Instances of performing multiple tasks incorporate paying attention to a web recording while at the same time answering an email or conversing with somebody via telephone while composing your report. Such performing multiple tasks hampers your capacity to concentrate as well as undermines your work quality.

Practice care and reflection. Thinking or rehearsing care exercises can fortify prosperity and mental wellness and further develop the center. During the contemplation cycle, our mind becomes quieter and our entire body turns out to be looser. We center around our breath during the interaction so we won't be occupied by our brains. With training, we can figure out how to utilize our breath to take our consideration back to a specific undertaking so it tends to be done well regardless of whether we get interfered with.

Get more rest. Many variables influence your rest. One of the most widely recognized is perusing from an electronic gadget like a PC, telephone, or tablet or watching your #1 film or Program on a Drove television not long before sleep time. Research has shown that such gadgets produce light towards the blue finish of the range. Such light will animate your eye retina and forestall the emission of melatonin that advances rest expectation in the cerebrum. Utilize a channel or "blue light" glasses to limit such blue light or stay away from all electronic gadgets before bed. Alternate ways of further developing rest incorporate keeping away from practice late in the day, remaining hydrated over the day, utilizing journaling or breathing activities to calm the psyche, and making an anticipated sleep time route

# Chapter 3

**THE ACTIVITY MINDSET**

What Is an Activity Mentality? An Essential for Progress

As the name proposes, an activity outlook is a mentality that is equipped for making a move. Individuals who have an activity-situated mentality don't trust that the powers of fate will line up or for the dream to visit. They make a move even in sub-par conditions because non-activity kills force.

The following are five mentalities that all activity-arranged individuals share for all intents and purposes.

What's the significance here to Have an Activity Situated Attitude?

Effective individuals will generally have an activity mentality — they have fostered the propensity for making a move in any event when things are somewhat flawed.

All activity-situated individuals will more often than not pronounce the accompanying five perspectives.

Nothing is truly going to be awesome, so don't trust that flawlessness will act.
Activity fixes endlessly dread is the thing that is preventing you from making a move.
Try not to sit tight for motivation. Simply begin acting, and motivation will come.
Think "presently," not "later."
Step up to the plate. Others will regard this.
1) Nothing Is Truly Going to Be Awesome
Numerous Passivationists need to trust that all that will be wonderful before they make a move. However, conditions, timing, and others are never going to be awesome.

Individuals won't ever be awesome.
A man in his late thirties needed to get hitched and have a family and an ideal life. He composed a prenup specifying everything from his future spouse's way of behaving to what sort

of companions they would have. His life partner recoiled and canceled it, saying "for better or in negative ways" was sufficient for her.
Fruitful individuals realize that individuals are flawed; taking care of unavoidable issues is worth the effort in connections.
The timing won't ever be great.
You and your accomplice fantasize about purchasing a house, yet you believe if you stand by, the market might get to the next level. Be that as it may, holding up may not be the response; it could be some unacceptable time later for different reasons.
Effective individuals think innovatively and track down ways of making their objectives, for example, purchasing a home, a reality in any event, when issues crop up.
Conditions won't ever be awesome.
You need to go with your family on a street outing when things are perfect. Be that as it may, on the off chance that you held on until conditions were great (climate, no terrible drivers, amazing streets), you'd never go.

Fruitful individuals face awful circumstances
and track down clever fixes. They don't trust that
conditions will be amazing before they make a
move.
Fruitful individuals make a move, meet issues as
they emerge, and sort out them innovatively en
route.

2) Activity Fixes Dread
At the point when we put off our objectives
since we're apprehensive about the likely
barricades ahead, we give our superb thoughts a
raw deal. These thoughts — what we might have
achieved — can catch up with us.

Dread prompts lost open doors and lament. The
creator alludes to this as the "apparition of
thoughts returning to cause major problems for
you."
Consider a capable essayist with a charming
voice and a convincing subject. On the off
chance that he lets dread and life disrupt the
general flow and never composes his book, he'll

feel tremendous lament for what could have been.

Fruitful individuals give their thoughts esteem by following up on them. At the point when they follow up on their thoughts they gain true serenity and certainty. There's no considering "what could have been" had they composed the book, beginning the business, purchased the property, or run the race. They are at this point not scared of the obscure because they know it. Activity annihilates dread and makes certainty.

Might it be said that you are fearing settling on a specific telephone decision? Settle on the decision and the trepidation is no more.

Fear going to the dental specialist? Coarseness your teeth (in a manner of speaking) and simply go. The apprehension that had been tormenting you is deleted and your certainty is reinforced.

3) Don't Sit tight for Motivation

Imagine a scenario where you are in an imaginative calling, like composition or workmanship. You might think you want motivation, to hang tight for the "soul to move you" to make a move.

In any case, motivation isn't required for activity, even in an imaginative undertaking. Fruitful individuals don't trust that the soul will move them; all things being equal, they move the soul. They hop right in and get rolling.

The way into this is a "mechanical methodology." Just do the activities that you want to, and the motivation will come.

On the off chance that an essayist isn't feeling propelled, yet has cutoff times to meet, she could simply begin composing, writing down any contemplations that ring a bell. Sometimes, her brain will refocus track, and coordinate, prodding inventive reasoning.
Consider a disagreeable errand that needs to finish (the dishes, calling a troublesome client). Presently quit mulling over everything — essentially hop right in and get rolling without consultation or fear.

Get a pencil and paper to write down a thought and guide out an arrangement. Recording your thought attaches your psyche to the thought all the more solidly and supports your focus, assisting you with bouncing beginning your soul to make the fundamental move.

4) Think "Presently," Not "Later"

"Presently" is an enchanted word — an expression of activity. Words, for example, "sometime in the not-so-distant future," "tomorrow," and "after this thing occurs," are expressions of inaction. Fruitful individuals are molded to make a move now.

Be motivated by the expressions of Benjamin Franklin: "Don't postpone until tomorrow what you can do today."

Need to send a very much past due card to say thanks? Plunk down, compose it and send it. Have a thought that could end up being useful to your business? Present it now.

Have you been pondering beginning a reserve
funds plan, however, expenses appear to be
excessively close. At any rate, begin it now.
Be careful with a typical propensity for inaction:
planning to act. Planning to act is a period
executioner that squanders valuable energy and
assets you could be utilizing to act at this
moment.

# Chapter 4

## HOW TO BE THE BIGGEST MOTIVATION TO MYSELF

Self-inspiration is the capacity to drive oneself to step up and activity to seek after objectives and complete errands. It's an inward drive to make a move — to make and to accomplish. It pushes you to continue onward on assignments, particularly those you're chasing after because you need to, not because somebody told you to.

While going after a major objective, self-inspiration assumes a key part. Yet, rolling out an improvement in your life requires tirelessness, and a large number of us find it hard to remain persuaded over the long haul.

When deciding to accomplish a drawn-out objective, whether it's to get sound, make a midlife vocation change, or understand an individual dream, the start is simple. You're loaded with imperativeness and assurance to confront the test.

In any case, large numbers of our most valuable objectives don't occur rapidly. It takes difficult work, constancy, and discipline to transform you. At the point when results don't come as fast as you expect, or when nothing goes right, it's normal to feel disappointed and experience issues remaining roused.

Investigating how to find inspiration will give the instruments to beat plunges, foster mental strength, work on your emphasis on your objectives, and keep you on a consistent way toward progress. So we should start!

What Is Self-Inspiration?
self-inspiration
To find inspiration, we first need to comprehend what we're truly referring to.

Inspiration is just the power driving your way of behaving. It's the "why" behind all that you do, and the explanation you could take up a reason. focus on an activity, or work toward an objective. All that we do is roused by a blend of cognizant and oblivious need or want.

At the point when we discuss self-inspiration, we are going past essential thought processes. What we truly mean is the capacity to finish rolling out an improvement throughout everyday life — without surrendering. Self-inspiration expects that you put stock in yourself, remain roused, and continue onward regardless of mishaps.

At the end of the day, we are discussing coarseness.

Analyst Angela Duckworth concentrated on the qualities of successful people and found that energy and diligence are the vital drivers of long-haul achievement. Coarseness takes you farther than the underlying thought process behind your objective after the buzz of fervor wears off. Coarseness takes you the entire way to the end goal.

Anyway, how might we figure out how to tackle these characteristics and foster self-inspiration to succeed?

What drives inspiration?
try not to surrender letter-blocks-on-corkboard
Albeit self-inspiration requires a drawn-out view, it's critical to see what is spurring you to look for change. The more clear you are on "why," the simpler it will be to remain fixed on the work you're doing, and to make the existence you need.

Once in a while thought processes can go unnoticed just by being casual, concealed inside the psyche, letting us know where it counts inside that something needs to change. Wants can develop, once in a while instantly of motivation, and in some cases through self-disclosure over the long run.

You'll make some more straightforward memories remaining spurred by perceiving the intentions behind your objectives. Becoming

mindful of these thought processes, and their
source, works on mindfulness while additionally
keeping you on target toward objectives that
genuinely make a difference to you.

Characteristic inspiration
Characteristic inspiration alludes to seeking after
an objective in light of inside factors.

As opposed to outer prizes, similar to cash or
acknowledgment, naturally persuaded activities
to have an underlying individual award.
Sensations of satisfaction, tracking down reason,
and accomplishing greatness comes from
chasing after characteristically inspired
objectives.

All in all, our most profound cravings, needs,
and dreams come from the inside and drive
self-inspiration.

A few instances of inborn inspiration incorporate
working on propensities to feel better, chasing
after a long-lasting fantasy about turning into a

craftsman or building more grounded, more significant associations with individuals.

What sincere longings drive you to improve personally and seek after your fantasies? That is where you will track down characteristic inspiration.

Extraneous inspiration
Extraneous inspiration connects with activities that we seek after in light of outside factors. On account of outward inspiration, we intend to achieve some sort of remuneration like cash, status, or great execution.

A few instances of extraneously spurred objectives are looking for ideal grades in school, hitting deals objectives at work, or changing your appearance to satisfy others.

What sort of drivers lead you to buckle down for substantial, quantifiable prizes? Those are your extraneous inspirations.

Everybody is unique, and in this way, every individual has their arrangement of natural or extraneous inspiration. Whether you feel more supported by interior inspiration or think of yourself as affected by the outside, or both, is correct or wrong.

All things considered, you need to make a point to perceive inspiration, so you can try not to pursue void objectives. After everything of a major accomplishment, you can't appreciate achievement when everything revolved around living another person's fantasy.

Tips to track down inspiration
do-what-you-love-inspirational
Change is difficult for anybody. Finding self-inspiration requires long-haul responsibility, fortitude, and persistence. In any case, that doesn't mean it's unthinkable. It essentially implies you need to track down ways of giving yourself a lift when you want it and abstain from surrendering when you hit a plunge.

Here are the most ideal ways to remain spurred, regardless of the amount you want to surrender:

1. Improve concentrate your energy
Making an existence of straightforwardness concerning self-inspiration will keep interruptions under control and keep you from feeling overpowered, particularly during seasons of progress. Effortlessness permits space in our minds and hearts to become imaginative and develop through difficulties.

Rather than attempting to seek after numerous objectives without a moment's delay, pick your area of concentration. This won't just assist with improving your life, however, will empower you to coordinate every one of your abilities toward your most significant objective. Expect to become boss in one region, rather than weakly working in numerous areas immediately.

2. Separate huge objectives into little advances
Investigate the bigger objective and consider the little moves toward accomplishing it. Break

everything into little, edible pieces so you can celebrate wins. As you celebrate, you'll set off dopamine discharge in your minds, a significant synthetic to keep up with inspiration.

Gamifying the interaction can assist with sectionalizing an enormous objective into possible undertakings so you can praise the little wins as you hit them. It's a typical propensity for fruitful individuals and functions admirably to make huge objectives more feasible.

3. Deal with your assumptions
At the point when you don't see improvement as fast as you expect, or you hit a tangle in your arrangements, the sensation of dissatisfaction is the most vital move towards surrendering. As hindrances stack up, disappointment becomes hopelessness, and you might tell yourself, "This objective isn't feasible."

Your cerebrum is continually working out whether it merits the work to continue onward. In the book Burnout, writers Emily Nagoski,

Ph.D., and Amelia Nagoski, DMA, refer to this idea as "The Screen." the cycle in your cerebrum keeps a running count of the work to advance proportion in any endeavor.

"The Screen" will in general have ridiculous assumptions.

There is consistently a dull evening of the spirit, and your nerves might debilitate. You ought to expect a plunge wherein force dials back or the direction appears to be unbalanced.

Your work in remaining persuaded is to track down ways of dealing with the pressure and personal unrest of the unavoidable plunges — and continue onward. You want to trust in yourself, and your abilities.

4. Encircle yourself with strong individuals
We should have individuals around us who assist us with keeping in contact with our ideal results. Individuals who have a huge emotionally supportive network or even one strong

individual in their corner, passage better than those going solo.

This is where the organization you keep becomes basic. We should have individuals who can connect with us, see us, and back us to remain positive.

In her top-of-the-line book, Conversational Knowledge, Judith E. Glazer makes sense of how steady individuals can step in to direct and propel us like a mentor during football match. During the round of life, in which we seek after our objectives, positive individuals can help you Rethink, Divert, and Pull together when it gets extreme.

Then again, an unsupportive climate triggers mental and actual trouble that crashes progress towards uplifting objectives.

5. Request help — and offer it
While you're attempting to remain roused in your mission, the right assist with canning is the

contrast between progress and surrendering. As indicated by Teacher Richard Boyatzis, who has read up on inspiration for quite a long time, we can all profit from turning out to be better at offering and getting the right sort of instruction.

The default type of assistance we with tending to offer is designated "training for consistency." It includes attempting to fix somebody or inspiring them to do what you need. Regardless of whether the counsel is sound, this approach doesn't attempt to make enduring positive change. The individual on the less-than-desirable end feels forced, and they don't learn a lot that will assist them with developing.

The methodology that works is classified as "instructing with sympathy." This training style isn't tied in with aiding, yet all the same about mindfulness. Discussions with incredible mentors tie your objectives back to your qualities and dreams. By adding a setting, they help self-inspiration and receptiveness to novel thoughts.

Do you know mindful, shrewd individuals in your circle that can uphold you through this difficult time? Maybe you are aware of somebody who has achieved the objectives you have decided to accomplish. If not, you can find support by getting a mentor, finding brain gathering, or joining a care group for individuals confronting a comparative test. Private venture mentors are devoted experts who have practical experience in assisting entrepreneurs and leaders with bettering accomplish their objectives.

6. Practice appreciation
While seeking after a major objective, it's not difficult to see your weaknesses and miss perceiving your accomplishments en route. This cynicism can kill self-inspiration. So make sure to perceive the endowments in you

# Chapter 5

**FOCUSING ON PROCESS BEFORE RESULTS**

A lot of creators explain to you WHY zeroing in on the cycle is great, yet not many let you know HOW to do that. This article will tell you BOTH.

For this book, I will separate things into 3 areas:

WHY zeroing in more on the cycle can be useful.

WHEN to zero in on the cycle and when to zero in on the result.

Instructions to zero in on the cycle (utilizing a 3-step Technique).

Note, this is the initial segment of a two-section series. After understanding this, make certain to look at Section 2: How to Figure out how to Partake All the while (11 Strategies)

Frame

1) Segment 1: Why Zeroing in More on the Cycle Can Be Useful

2) Segment 2: When to Zero in on the Cycle and When to Zero in on the Result
3) Segment 3: How to Zero in on the Cycle (Utilizing a 3-Step Strategy)
4) Last Contemplations

Area 1: Why Zeroing in More on the Cycle Can Be Useful

A great many people invest considerably an excess of energy pondering WHERE they need to get concerning their objectives.

What's more, not anywhere close to sufficient time on the Particular Advances it will take to contact them.

Society helps us to find true success, you want to obtain results.

In any case, society doesn't necessarily stress that to obtain the best outcomes, you want to zero in more on the cycle.

Furthermore, not exclusively will zeroing in more on the cycle get you the outcomes you are searching for, but it will likewise make you a ton more joyful.

For instance, assuming you are considering,
there are two approaches:
Result-Centered Approach: Considering to
arrive at a specific wanted outcome. For
instance, getting a passing mark in a class you
are taking or excelling on a test.
Process-Centered Approach: Zeroing in on the
particular cycles included, for example,
accepting notes as you are perusing, doing
rehearse issues, retaining data, or essentially
giving close consideration to the perusing
material itself.
There are four justifications for why zeroing in
more on the cycle can get you improved results.

Reason 1: It Assists You With focusing on the
Job needing to be done
Envision you are examining and are completely
caught up in the thing you are doing. What's
more, not getting continually occupied by
considerations like "I truly want to believe that I
excel on this test."

At the point when you are profoundly centered around something, your presentation improves considerably.

In this way, focusing closer on the cycle will assist you with getting in that profoundly engaged attitude.

Reason 2: It Makes it Simpler to Recognize Valuable open doors for Development

As you center around the interaction more, you become more mindful of which explicit parts are working out positively and which are not.

This expanded mindfulness empowers you to recognize open doors for development.

If your brain holds floating to the outcome, it will not be as simple for you to review every one of the little subtleties and how to change them. However, assuming you are completely submerged in the thing you are doing, you will see things you probably won't have known about in any case.

For instance, say you are figuring out how to play the guitar, and your psyche is centered around the result.

Maybe you want to significantly improve to the point of beginning a band.

On the off chance that you are occupied with wandering off in fantasy land about beginning a band while playing, you probably won't get on unobtrusive things about your method that you could refine.

Like not holding down a portion of the notes sufficiently in specific harmonies.

Be that as it may, assuming you center around the interaction while rehearsing, you are bound to get on those little open doors for development.

Which will prompt more proficient advancement toward your objectives.

Reason #3: Zeroing in on the Cycle Makes Chasing after Your Objective More Agreeable
On the off chance that you center around the cycle, you are bound to find natural awards in anything you are doing.

Characteristic prizes are benefits you get as a trade-off for the work you do which come from the inside.

For example:
The fulfillment from standing by listening to the guitar as you play.
Or on the other hand, the feeling of achievement as you begin to sort out another PC program.
At the point when you are process-centered, you are focusing harder on these sorts of things.

Furthermore, hence are Bound to find parts of pursuing your objective that you genuinely appreciate.

Side note - I have a full article on natural prizes versus outward rewards
Reason #4: It Assists You With adhering to Your Objectives
It does this in two ways:

In the first place, as you figure out how to find things characteristically agreeable about your interest, it will make it simpler for you to stay aware of your objectives. That is because you are bound to stay with something you appreciate. Second, most objectives can consume a large chunk of the day to achieve. On the off chance that you simply center around the result, you could get deterred because you're not accomplishing your objective adequately fast. Nonetheless, it is substantially more reassuring to zero in on the cycle. That is because you are centered around the little, individual parts of your objective.

Also, those easily overlooked details are substantially more attainable in the short run.

Area 2: When to Zero in on the Cycle and When to Zero in on the Result
To best make sense of this, I will split things into three stages:

The Arranging Stage: When you plan, examine, and believe through how best to arrive at your objective.

The Execution Stage: When you effectively carry out the means expected to accomplish your objective.

The Estimation Stage: When you intermittently evaluate the headway you are making towards your objective.

Stage 1: The Arranging Stage

Here you research how you want to achieve your objective and plan out the particular advances required.

In the Arranging Stage, you need to zero in less on the result, and more on the cycle.

At the point when you initially choose to seek after something, you for the most part have a result as a primary concern.

For instance, your objective may be to figure out how to cook, run a long-distance race, or begin a business.

Having these goals is thoroughly fine. What's more, normally, you must contemplate your

ultimate objective a tad during the arranging
stage.
To sort out some way to best accomplish it.
In any case, when you center A lot around the
ultimate objective, that can prompt unclear, wide
plans, which aren't considered completely.

What's more, it's harder to finish when you don't
have an unmistakable vision at the top of the
priority list.

In any case, assuming that your arrangement is
more unambiguous, and process-centered,
executing your plans will be simpler.

Suggested Article: How to Separate Objectives
Into Steps

Stage 2: The Execution Stage
The Execution Stage is the point at which you
carry out the means expected to accomplish your
objective.

For instance, if you want to compose a book, this is the stage after you've arranged your story, and presently are composing.

The Execution Stage is where it is Generally vital to zero in on the cycle and not the outcome.

That is for two reasons:
To start with, it further develops execution. At the point when you are executing an errand, you need to be in the zone, profoundly focusing on executing the particular cycles included. Zeroing in on the result at this stage is only an interruption from the job needing to be done.
Second, zeroing in on the cycle makes the action more agreeable.
That is because zeroing in on the cycle assists you with remaining right now, which lessens the uneasiness and stress you get when you are daydreaming, agonizing over the outcome.

Additionally, when you focus on the interaction as you are making it happen, you are bound to find things you like about it.

Stage 3: The Estimation Stage

In the Estimation Stage, you evaluate your advancement toward your objective and refine things if necessary.

At this stage, it assists with gauging your advancement in light of a blend of cycle and result.

During the estimation stage, you need to think about the result, since you want to decide the amount of progress you have made toward your objective. Like that, you can sort out whether any changes are required.

In any case, you additionally need to think about the cycle, since you want to pinpoint the regions that need improvement. To upgrade your presentation later on.

Segment 3: How to Zero in on the Cycle (Utilizing a 3-Step Strategy)

This technique is to zero in less on the outcome and more on the actual cycle, by finding things you like about the interaction.

Remember, this technique is fundamentally intended to assist with the Execution Stage (the stage when zeroing in on the process is generally significant).

Side note I have made a free aide which examines how to zero in on the cycle in different stages too. (More data on this toward the finish of the article).

To make it simpler to track, I will involve concentrating, as an illustration, all through. (Yet, this can apply to any objective!)

Stage 1: Find Something You Like About the Interaction
Perhaps the most compelling motivation it very well may be difficult to zero in on the cycle is that there are many times negatives in the process that consume your psyche.

With examination, there are a lot of potential negatives included, including:

The extreme focus is expected to peruse and
hold data.
The pressure that happens about whether we will
do well in a class or on a test.
Culpability over tarrying and not having
concentrated before.
The tension from society, family, and friends to
do competently.
Furthermore, at times, an abhorrence of the
material.
So how would you fix this?

To begin with, begin by finding a piece of
something you like simultaneously.

Regardless of whether it is a staggeringly little
part, that is fine.

Furthermore, remember, this is only an
exploratory stage, so no strain to sort it out
immediately.

While considering, there are likewise numerous expected upsides. For instance:

The fulfillment of realizing you are obtaining new information.
The interest in learning new or fascinating material.
Furthermore, the inclination that you are achieving something useful.
Continue to deal with this step until you've found somewhere around one component you like about anything that you are doing.

Stage 2: Focus on the Angle You Like
Now that you've found something you like, begin focusing on that viewpoint whenever the situation allows.

You might need to rehearse this for a couple of days, before continuing toward Stage 3.

Stage 3: When Your Brain Floats, Return to the Perspectives You Like

Presently, at whatever point your brain meanders and starts contemplating the result. Or on the other hand about parts of the interaction, you could do without. Attempt to Move your consideration back to pondering the things you LIKE.

# Chapter 6

**LEARNING TO PLAN AND EXECUTE**

Assuming that you've as of late been entrusted with executing a change drive, or are attempting to sort out why your association's last procedure neglected to be carried out, you may know that you're following some great people's example. Finishing things — executing both association-wide systems and more modest drives — is interesting at many organizations. Contingent upon where you look, the execution disappointment rate is somewhere in the range of 65 to 90 percent. It's to be expected, then, that a study of more than 400 worldwide Chiefs uncovered that an absence of execution greatness was their top test, demolishing development, international precariousness, and top-line development.

Knowing those grim numbers, you might have chosen to dive in and figure out how and why others fizzled. You will not need to look far: a new Google search concocted "Three

Motivations behind Why Great Techniques Fizzle," "Why System Execution Falls flat (4 Normal Issues)," "Five Reasons Most Organizations Come up short at Methodology Execution," and even "10 Justifications for Why Organizations Neglect to Execute their Procedures" — to give some examples.

There's no lack of counsel, at the same time, says Wharton The executive's teacher Nicolaj Siggelkow, "there's just such a lot of you can do with an article. Everybody recognizes that most drives fizzle — procedures with a capital S, however more modest drives as well. To truly make a mark, and have an impact on how you handle the execution, you can't simply depend on perusing."

Siggelkow says the high pace of disappointment is "precisely why we have the extended Successful Execution of Authoritative Methodology program. Everybody battles with execution, whether you're a business, an administration office, or a charity." The uplifting news is you can figure out how to succeed. The program is an involved studio that tends to every one of the critical hindrances to execution. Grounded in research, it uses crafted by seven Wharton teachers who show in the school's MBA program.

Members bring a real execution challenge from their work environment and go through the week applying what they are figuring out how to that test. That begins with recognizing and figuring out how to address possible hindrances. Then, the center moves to make energy for new drives. Siggelkow has members sort out each individual they need to converse with, inside and outside the association, and afterward create the right message.

"You might have to have various directives for various individuals. Not every person will become amped up for how you outline it to engage those in finance, for instance," he says. "Furthermore, those external to your capability and specialty unit might have contending interests so you want to present the defense in a manner that impacts them. Yet, fundamental to these messages is a comprehension of the company's procedure so you can suggest a compelling case for how the drive helps it."

Over time, members work with and gain from one another. "This is one of the extraordinary upsides of an open enlistment program," says Siggelkow. "At industry occasions, the learning is restricted, and firms don't talk straightforwardly when a contender might be in the room. Compelling Execution draws a global cross-segment of pioneers from a scope of ventures and non-business associations, and as they share their difficulties, they get input from one another. It very well may be educational to figure out that somebody working at an administration organization in the Center East or Africa is managing similar sorts of issues you are."

The week closes with a Procedure Execution studio that arranges the structures that have been all common in the class. Members apply them to the venture they carried with them and foster a definite methodology for tending to it. "Toward the day's end," Siggelkow says, "the week's examples are both pragmatic and significant. They accompany an issue and leave with an arrangement close by that they can begin utilizing on Monday morning."

# Chapter 7

**TAKING MEANINGFUL RISKS**

We should discuss risk-taking. Be that as it may, before we continue, we should move a certain something: assuming you're understanding this (or paying attention to the web recording) — it's reasonable you need to turn out to be to a greater extent a daring person throughout everyday life. I'm certain you would rather not begin facing challenges out of the blue; but since there's a hole between where you are presently and where you need to be.

At this moment in time, you may think, "no kidding, stupid, that I'm hanging around for." Yet a few of us aren't stopped certain assuming that turning into a daring person is pretty much as productive as all the messy self-improvement masters let us know in their siphon up-discourses… So we should be forthright about it: Turning into a daring person isn't ideal for everybody. Assuming you're uncertain about whether increasing your gamble-taking game is the right move for you, then, at that point, you might need to continue toward something different. Since convincing you to turn into a daring person isn't the motivation behind this article/episode. All things considered, this piece is for you on the off chance that you've previously decided — you right now accept you want to turn out to be to a greater extent a daring person — to accomplish a more significant level of progress throughout everyday life.

The motivation behind this piece, then, at that point, is to show you — or perhaps remind you — the stuff to turn into a fruitful daring individual, addressing all parts of life, yet primarily centering inside the setting of building an effective vocation/business accomplishing significant work. However, paying little mind to what your identity is, where you're at, or what you do, you'll have the option to decipher these thoughts on risk-taking and apply them in your own life. Things being what they are, we should make a plunge, will we?

Daring person TIP 1: BE Ludicrously Nonsensical.

At the point when I quit my comfortable corporate gig to begin living the dream and getting paid for the privilege — which is to rouse significance in individuals all over the place — I took a significant, significant gamble. For instance, when I began FlashBooks I scarcely had sufficient in the bank to help my way of life for over 90 days!

In those days, I scarcely had adequate room in my condo to telecommute. So how did I respond? I contributed a lump of my assets to a quality MacBook Ace. Then I changed over my kitchen into an office-space-cut studio to record book recording synopses and digital broadcast episodes.

In addition, leaving my place of employment to pursue my calling likewise implied I needed to:

get another vehicle (since the one I had — an organization vehicle — wasn't exactly mine in any case)

start creating sufficient income to help myself before I began seeing an excessive number of openings in my (generally small) 3-month security net to continue onward. Also, last but surely not least, I realized I'd need to…

put it all out there harder than I at any point had — regardless — all while arriving at savvy conclusions about what to zero in on (lucrative open doors) and what to disregard.

This is upsetting stuff we're discussing here. No authentic person of normal insight would follow through with something like this assuming they were thinking judiciously. Concentrates on a show that the more brilliant you are, the more gamble unfriendly you are. Why? Since sane reasoning assists you with deciding how advantageous and significant another endeavor (also known as risk) will or won't be. Along these lines, on the off chance that you were pondering gamble-taking, you could say:

I'm as of now making $XYZ each year. Without a doubt, I don't cherish my work, however, I have a few weighty bills to pay

Consider the possibility that I don't succeed. What if I fizzle? Consider the possibility that I screw up and embarrass myself. What will individuals think?

Perhaps beginning that business is not a smart thought all things considered.

Unendingly and on… Presently every one of the levelheaded, impeccably legitimized motivations not to turn into a daring person begin streaming into your outskirts and start obfuscating your judgment; squashing your fantasies for a superior future, as Donald Trump's official mission. In what would seem like no time, you've persuaded yourself that it's an ill-conceived notion to face that challenge. That it's smarter to remain safe — to remain judicious.
Yet, being ludicrously silly is an alternate story.

It isn't tied in with "thinking positive" and declining to recognize the real factors of a given circumstance to Be strangely nonsensical. Being incredibly silly is tied in with being unreasonably hopeful about what's in store. It's tied in with fostering a dream and utilizing that vision to assist you with gathering up the — boldness/energy/power — anything that it takes, to persevere until you succeed.

Be that as it may, why go on when you continue to tumble down? Since…

Daring person TIP 2: An Effective Daring individual IS A Momentary Doubter AND A Drawn out Positive thinker.

I recall when it was truly getting right down to the last possible second for me. At the point when I was attempting to sort out a method for supporting my fantasies and accomplishing significant work. I recollect how I continued to attempt many thoughts, getting super-amped up for every one of them, just to watch them fizzle, each right in succession. It seemed like nothing would work.

Yet, for reasons unknown, I realized it would end up working. I knew it in my center. In addition to the fact that I knew I'd be OK, I realized I'd find actual success. It would simply require somewhat more investment. What amount of additional time? I didn't have the foggiest idea. Furthermore, you will not by the same token. Be that as it may, what you in all actuality do have to know is this:

A large portion of the stuff you attempt — the majority of the dangers you take — won't work. Furthermore, that is fine. Since what doesn't work today, will lead you towards what functions admirably tomorrow. — Snap to-Tweet

As far as I might be concerned, it wasn't necessary to focus on what didn't work yesterday, or what's not working today. It would work tomorrow. It's forever been that way for me, and I can't highlight one explicit defining moment that made me change my outlook toward this course. In any case, I realize it works. Turn into a momentary doubter and a drawn-out confident person. It'll pay off. Believe me.

Daring person TIP 3: DON'T Pay attention TO DREAM Executioners.
I recollect each one around me continued advising me to quit trying and simply find a standard line of work like "every other person." I advised them to fuck off.

I'd made a guarantee to myself that I could never permit myself to become subjugated by any individual or organization in return for a check at any point down the road. I'd much prefer to serve individuals in a significant manner, doing something important to me.

You can do the same thing. Try not to let dream executioners keep you from accomplishing your objectives. You encapsulate significance. Furthermore, YOU are answerable for imparting that significance to the world. Try not to let

dream executioners squash your motivation.
Reduce most, if not all, connections with them.
Furthermore, if your fantasy executioners are
individuals you end up cherishing and care for,
make the expectation of returning to help them
out once you're sufficiently able to do as such.
At this moment, however, you should be
centered around encircling yourself with rousing
and empowering individuals and things. Things
like the accompanying little chunk of astuteness
composed by the well-known writer, Neil
Simon:

"Try not to pay attention to the people who say
'you taking too enormous a risk.' Michelangelo
would have painted the Sistine floor, and it
would most likely be wiped out by today.
Generally significant, don't listen when the little
voice of dread inside you reappears and says
'they generally more astute than you out there.
They're more skilled, they're taller, blonder,
prettier, more fortunate, and they have
associations." I solidly trust that assuming you
follow a way that intrigues you, not to the

prohibition of affection, responsiveness, and participation with others, but with the strength of conviction that you can move others independently — and don't make achievement or disappointment the models by which you live — the odds are you'll be your very own individual deserving regards."

Daring person TIP 4: YOUR Prosperity WILL BE IN DIRECT Extent TO THE Gamble THEY'RE WILLING TO TAKE.
At the point when you approach the madly alluring young lady/fellow at the shopping center and make proper acquaintance — you're taking a significant, significant gamble. In any case, consider the possibility that s/he's "the one."

At the point when you choose to stroll into the rec center and begin working out — paying little heed to how fat or wobbly you look contrasted to all the others — you're taking a significant, significant gamble. In any case, shouldn't something be said about all the energy, essentialness, and actual changes you'll get to appreciate with your new rec center propensity?

At the point when you choose to leave your place of employment and go out on a limb — you're taking a significant, significant gamble. However, shouldn't something be said about the way of life that accompanies taking care of business you find satisfying?

How much achievement you experience will extend — or recoil — to a direct extent to how much gamble you're willing to take.

I've in a real sense 10X'd my I come since I quit my place of employment and go into business. Furthermore, that is only the monetary advantage I've encountered because of making a "dangerous" profession move… When I stop to think about the wide range of various advantages — the close to home, social, and profound effect that taking care of the business I love has had on my life — I thoroughly comprehend that the gamble was justified. Thinking back now, it was very nearly an easy decision.

Gracious, and incidentally: I'm not expressing any of this to intrigue you, but rather to present for you that our prosperity grows to the level of hazard we're willing to take…

80% of the time, the more you're willing to risk, the more you're possibly going to get consequently. Also, that goes two different ways — negative and positive. Once again, only just in case: how much achievement you experience will grow — or shrivel — concerning the measure of a chance you're willing to take.

Daring person TIP 5: BECOME Effective BY Fostering A Development Outlook…
Effective daring people comprehend the conspicuous thought that hotshot risk-taking has its potential gains and disadvantages. Also, the disadvantages — like committing errors or falling flat at things — can truly suck now and

again. However, this is which isolates
individuals that thrive from individuals that die:

Attitude

People that prevail, again and again, have what's
known as a Development Outlook. Individuals
that appear to continue to stall out throughout
everyday life — ordinarily because they're
keeping themselves down — have what's known
as a Proper Mentality.

What's a Decent Mentality? As Hymn Dweck
places it in her (very amazing and
mind-extending) book, Attitude:

"Accepting that your characteristics are cut in
stone — the decent mentality — makes a

# Chapter 8

## MAKING RIGHT DECISIONS THAT ATTAIN SUCCESS

Review the most troublesome choice(s) you've looked at in your grown-up life: Picking a medical care plan, arranging your wedding, finding employment elsewhere, going into business, or sorting out the amount you want to put something aside for retirement.

Dynamic assumes a significant part in the manner situation transpire in our lives. However, individuals don't ordinarily give a lot of consideration to the significant impacts of simply deciding. The vast majority of us travel through life carelessly regarding what contemplations we're thinking and what moves we're making.

In any case, the everyday choices we make, make our very own world. What's more, our choices shape our identity as people.

The majority of us are modified to go with choices in light of dread, low confidence, and an absence of self-discipline.

So rather than taking striking actions, we end up caught in a safe place.

Fortunately, it's deductively demonstrated to be feasible to reconstruct your cerebrum for more elevated levels of awareness. In this way, on the off chance that you're disappointed with the status quo creating in your life at present, putting forth a purposeful attempt to move out of the safe place — to pursue better choices — will be the way to being the individual you need to be and making the existence you need to have from now on.

At the point when you put forth the attempt to assume command over your well-being, riches, and way of life in a positive way, you enact four neurological cycles, which co-creator of Neuro Shrewdness: The New Mind Study of Cash, Joy, and Achievement, Imprint Waldman alludes to as the "4 Mainstays of Riches." they are right here:

Inspiration. At the point when you become mindful of what interestingly propels you, you can intentionally pick the exercises that will bring the best achievement.

Independent direction. Whenever you are persuaded to gain or follow through with something, your cerebrum enacts circuits the cerebrums to begin deciding. This cycle can be upset by pressure, stress, and uncertainty. In any case, you can prepare your brain to remain on track, certain, and hopeful.

Innovativeness. Utilizing the powers of your innovative creative mind, you will take care of issues all the more rapidly and increment your efficiency.

Mindfulness. The course of careful self-reflection can upgrade mindfulness, social mindfulness, and profound mindfulness, providing your life with serious importance and motivation. You will likewise invigorate your mind's hardware for sympathy, empathy, and profound quality.

Every one of the over four points of support is fundamental for objective accomplishment and achievement. What's more, assuming you disregard any of them, you'll probably restrict your capacity to create both internal and external financial momentum.

How about we keep on zeroing in on the second mainstay of the four points of support: navigation? The following are eight moves to assist you with pursuing better choices.

1. Utilize the two sides of your cerebrum.
What is the most important phase in the dynamic cycle? All things considered, while pursuing a major choice, feel enabled to utilize the two sides of your cerebrum (rather than simply your legitimate, left side). Finding harmony between feeling and reason is significant.

The right cerebrum, our ability to understand people on a profound level, is naturally connected to our way of behaving . . . furthermore, the significant choices we make all through our lifetime. ~ Snap TO TWEET ~

Both your direction and thought-creating processes start in your left prefrontal cortex, and on the off chance that there isn't sufficient feeling behind these cycles, the piece of your cerebrum called the core accumbens (NAc) doesn't actuate. On the off chance that the NAc isn't actuated, dopamine (the vibe great synapse that perceives reward) will not be delivered into your body, and you'll probably stay unmotivated back in your usual range of familiarity. Also, choices produced using the safe place seldom wind up helping you over the long haul.

2. Envision your future, effective self.
To know how to go with effective choices, pause for a minute to ponder how achievement affects you. How would you characterize individual achievement? Record your response in a diary or on a piece of paper.

Then, picture your ideal, future self. Do this by getting into a casual position, shutting your eyes, and permitting your psyche to meander into a fantasy.

What do you see and feel? Could it be said that
you are radiating with energy? Do you have a
solid gleam about you? Could it be said that you
are in the best shape of all time? Is it true or not
that you are enamored? Do you have a strong
local area and a tomfoolery circle of friends?
Are you monetarily free? Do you coexist well
with your colleagues, partners, and workers?
Take notes, assuming you'd like.

Imaginative perception is a significant strategy
for any among us on the way to incredible
achievement. At the point when you have a
positive mental picture . . . what's more, see
yourself as an effective individual, you start to
accept you're equipped for wonderful
well-being, satisfaction, and riches. Truth can be
stranger than fiction, correct? What's more, you
should have the confidence to accomplish.

3. Perceive the power behind every choice you
make.

Before you settle on a choice, you need to figure out your preferred impacts. Any choice that you make makes a chain of occasions occur.

For instance, if an organization you'd very much want to work for requires you do a show for key partners before you're recruited . . . what's more, you choose not to proceed with it since you have apprehension about open talking, that choice could bring about you passing up a valuable chance to have your extravagant organization later on.

For this situation, everything reduces to first settling on the choice to conquer your apprehension about open talking, so you can live life to the fullest and be monetarily free until the end of your life.

4. Go with your stomach.
At the point when you end up faltering between numerous choices, your instinct is one of your most remarkable dynamic apparatuses. To focus on your hunch, stop briefly and don't ponder the

upsides and downsides . . . essentially sit in a tranquil spot and notice what sentiments rise to the top.

Do you feel tight in the chest region? Or on the other hand an open gentility in your heart? Do you feel alleviation? Fervor? What other actual sensations do you feel?

Research shows that our senses frequently first hit us on an instinctive level, letting us know what we want to realize a long time before our cognizance gets up to speed. Neuroscientist, and one of the world's driving experts on human awareness, Dr. Joel Pearson, late found that instinct in all actuality does exist.

Pearson and his examination group have exhibited that oblivious feelings work on the speed and exactness of navigation — a disclosure that could demonstrate significance for examinations concerning how cognizant and oblivious data consolidate to shape and impact ways of behaving.

While settling on enormous choices, you must tune into your internal insight. The best old guidance for sorting out what you genuinely need is to search inside.

So before taking any significant actions, carve out an opportunity to investigate that "interesting" feeling. You've doubtlessly suspected previously; a notion that guided you in the correct course? That is your intuition speaking with you. Focus on it.

Be still and know.

5. Try not to ask others what you ought to do. You don't need to ask individuals about their thought processes. It makes it significantly more challenging to settle on a choice when you are up to speed on others' perspectives about what's best for you.

Assuming you ask 4 individuals what they figure you ought to do, you will undoubtedly get 4 distinct tirades of counsel. Furthermore, the criticism will probably prompt disarray and rethinking.

Go ahead and counsel individuals who will be straightforwardly impacted by your choice . . . and afterward unhesitatingly let everybody in on what you've chosen.

6. Pose yourself with the right inquiries.
When you know how you feel about the choice, now is the right time to pose your mind the right inquiries: What is it that I need in this lifetime? Will the result of my choice draw me nearer to what I care about? Does the advantage offset the expense? Is the degree of chance worth the award? How committed am I to this change?

As Dr. David Welch, teacher of political theory at the College of Waterloo in Ontario and creator of Choices, Choices: The Specialty of Successful Navigation, makes sense, "Individuals who aren't self-intelligent will wind up pursuing terrible choices since they don't have any idea what they need in any case."

Before you seal the deal, ask yourself: Do I truly need to wed this individual? Or then again do I simply need to be hitched with kids sometime in the future?

7. Adjust your life to your fundamental beliefs. Choices you make because of your guiding principle make persuasive arrangements. So settle on your choices in light of whether they line up with your most elevated values, interests, and needs, or it won't feel like you pursued the ideal decision.

Before you can sort out whether or not the choice is joined with the things that mean the most to you, you first need to become clear about what those values are. Make a composed rundown of your most noteworthy qualities. Furthermore, when you're clear, make a rundown of the relative multitude of ways your decision adjusts (or doesn't line up) with those qualities.

8. Anything you choose to do, have coarseness and zeal.

Have you at any point met a dirty individual you could have done without? Regardless of whether you have, would you say you weren't to some degree in wonderment of their drive to succeed?

With regards to making a move in your life, you must have serious areas of strength for a. So before you go into business, ensure you're doing something that inspires you to continue (despite disappointment).

Coarseness is enthusiasm and constancy for extremely long-haul objectives. Coarseness is having endurance. Coarseness is staying with your future, all day, every day, not only for the week, for the month, but for quite a long time, and striving to make that future a reality. Coarseness is carrying on day-to-day life like it's a long-distance race, not a run.

Alongside coarseness, having zeal is a similarly significant characteristic of fruitful individuals. You must be energetic about the existing decisions you make. There's power in enthusiasm.

So with regards to pursuing the ideal choice, don't fall once more into the safe place and remain in a vocation you can't stand. Track down ways of starting up your soul and take monster jumps toward your fantasies.

At the point when you have energy and persistence for your drawn-out objectives, you can achieve anything